THE ROYAL HORTICULTURAL SOCIETY
PRACTICAL GUIDES

# OUTDOOR
# LIVING

D1333961

# THE ROYAL HORTICULTURAL SOCIETY
## PRACTICAL GUIDES

# OUTDOOR LIVING

## STEVEN BRADLEY

A Dorling Kindersley Book

Dorling **DK** Kindersley

LONDON, NEW YORK, SYDNEY, DELHI,
PARIS, MUNICH and JOHANNESBURG

PROJECT EDITOR Simon Maughan
DESIGNER Janice English

SERIES EDITOR Annelise Evans
SERIES ART EDITOR Ursula Dawson

MANAGING EDITOR Anna Kruger
MANAGING ART EDITOR Lee Griffiths

DTP DESIGNERS Louise Paddick, Louise Waller

PRODUCTION MANAGER Sarah Coltman

First published in Great Britain in 2001
by Dorling Kindersley Limited,
9 Henrietta Street,
Covent Garden, London WC2E 8PS

2 4 6 8 10 9 7 5 3 1

Copyright © 2001 Dorling Kindersley Limited

A CIP catalogue for this book is available from the British Library.
ISBN 0 7513 1296 7

Reproduced by Colourscan, Singapore
Printed and bound by Star Standard Industries PTE Ltd, Singapore

see our complete
catalogue at

# www.dk.com

# CONTENTS

# THE GARDEN AS AN OUTDOOR ROOM

## WHY CREATE AN OUTDOOR ROOM?

OVER RECENT YEARS, there has been an increasing preoccupation with spending more leisure time outdoors, particularly in the garden. This is a reaction to our changing lifestyle, both at work and at home. With more people working indoors than ever before, it is only natural that they spend as much leisure time as possible outside. On fine days, meals can be enjoyed in the garden, where they always seems to taste better and are eaten at a more relaxed pace.

### CHANGING ATTITUDES

As the average dwelling becomes smaller, there is a tendency to treat the garden as an outdoor room, and it is possible to equip it with shelter, outdoor furniture, and outdoor lighting, all designed to extend the time spent in the garden.

For most families, the garden must provide an area for playing as well as relaxing. Safety is a major consideration, particularly where young children are concerned. Close to a busy road, the garden is an essential place for children to play where they are under the discreet observation of their parents.

SHELTERED SUMMER *Not all garden-based pastimes are active. For some, a beautiful garden offers a quiet place to sit and read, or just relax and watch nature at work. A permanent shelter, such as this summer house, can greatly enhance the time spent outdoors.*

◀ ENTERTAINING OUTSIDE *Practical and atmospheric lights bring evening gatherings to life.*

# PLANNING AN OUTDOOR ROOM

T HE FIRST STAGE OF PLANNING is to decide what pastimes and activities you would like to use the garden for. If you have children, their needs will probably be your first and most major consideration. A garden that has been divided into rooms often seems bigger and more alluring, because concealed areas retain a sense of seclusion and mystery. It also offers the opportunity to create spaces tailored to different uses, each with a distinct mood.

## SEATING AND DINING AREAS

In an ideal garden, seating and dining areas are positioned in a sunny position as close to the house as possible. Such a site offers maximum convenience when preparing, cooking, and serving food, and it can be made into an extension of the house by adding a roof in the form of an awning, umbrella, or more permanent canopy.

If the sunny part of the garden is some distance away from the house, consider building the main seating area there. It

VERANDAH WITH A VIEW
*An area for relaxation can be many things; this verandah is the perfect place to sit and watch over life in the garden.*

may be a little less convenient, but a short walk is better than sitting in shade. On an exposed site, a screen may be essential to provide shelter from strong winds.

## STORAGE SITES

Many of us do not have the luxury of a large garden, so a single area must be adapted to fit several uses. Storage is perhaps the biggest problem, yet this is overcome easily with some imagination. The dead space beneath a raised floor of a shed, gazebo, or deck, for example, is usually forgotten, but with a hinged panel in the floor, tools, furniture, and toys can be placed out of sight and brought out when they are needed.

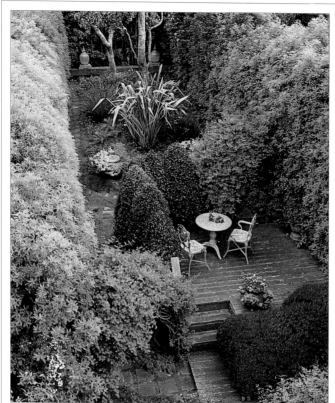

◀ SECLUDED SPACES
*If size permits, divide the garden into a number of separate, but linked, areas – like the rooms of a house. Use trellises, plants, hedges, or fences as dividers, in place of walls.*

▼ CONVERSATION PIT
*Not all gardens are built on a flat, level site, and this may appear to be a disadvantage at first. However, by combining raised beds with sunken paved areas, the lower level can be used to create an intimate area for conversation.*

## AREAS FOR CHILDREN

The most popular area for children of all ages is likely to be a open expanse of lawn as a general games area. Siting this away from the house, if possible, reduces noise

> A mature tree is the most obvious place for a play house or swing

and the risk of balls hitting house windows. If there is a mature tree in the garden, it would be the obvious place for a play house or swing. A tree used in this way also solves a common gardening problem, as the most difficult area to grow plants tends to be under the canopy of a large tree.

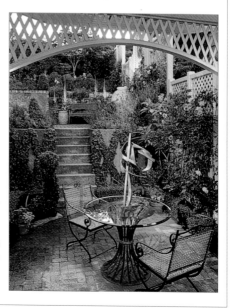

# EATING AND ENTERTAINING

A COMMON FEATURE OF OUTDOOR ENTERTAINING tends to be the large number of people dining. Eating *al fresco* seems to be more of a social gathering than a meal indoors, and it often involves one or two barbecues, a large table or several smaller ones, lots of seats, a source of heat, and some well-positioned candles, lanterns, or electric lights (*see pp.20–23*).

## THE CHOICE OF FURNITURE

There is a bewildering range of outdoor furniture on the market, in all styles, sizes, and qualities, and at all sorts of prices. If it is intended to be outdoors all year, rigid furniture is probably the best choice, but the real problem is which to choose. As well as choosing items in a style and colour that will suit the garden's design – be it modern or traditional – you will need to consider the practical aspects.

For durability and ease of maintenance, plastic furniture is very popular. It requires no painting or weatherproofing, although some cheaper types become brittle after several years of exposure to bright sunlight. Plastic furniture can look out of place in a very traditional setting, but its clean lines and bright colours are well suited to modern or family gardens.

Metal garden furniture is less commonly seen, although there are some innovative contemporary steel seats and tables available, and some very good copies of traditional wrought- or cast-ironwork. This type of furniture is often very ornamental as well as functional, but iron will need maintenance, such as washing down and painting (*see p.76*), and it can be uncomfortable to sit on for long periods.

BREAKFAST
IN THE SUN
*In a small garden, fold-away tables and chairs are a wise option, since they take up little storage space in winter, and they are easy to move about. Here, the furniture has been positioned to catch the morning sun.*

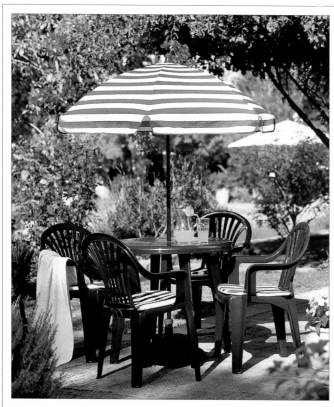

A POPULAR CHOICE
*There is much to recommend the use of plastic furniture in outdoor areas. It is comfortable, lightweight, easily wiped clean, and affordable. Many colours are available, so co-ordinating furniture with the garden's design will not be difficult.*

On the other hand, there is aluminium, which has all of the good qualities of other types of metal furniture, but with the advantages of being light and easy to store.

Both plastic and metal furniture can be cold to sit on at times, and very hot during high summer; the temperature of wood or

> ## The bright colours of plastic furniture suit modern gardens

wicker remains much more constant. The longevity of wood ultimately depends on the quality and how well it is maintained, especially in terms of weather-proofing (*see p.76*). Wooden garden furniture can be very heavy, but it is usually comfortable to sit

on, and many people do prefer its natural feel. Choose from hardwood or treated softwood; both types can be stained or painted, if required, so that the furniture matches, or contrasts with, the rest of the garden, such as a neighbouring trellis, fence, or planting display.

## SETTING THE MOOD

• When setting the table, make simplicity your goal and concentrate on comfort.
• Site a raised bed planted with fragrant herbs close to an eating area; the edge of the bed can be a good place to sit and talk.
• Decorate an entertaining area with flowers, for scent and colour at different levels, from beds and pots to hanging baskets.
• Use lighting to create pools of light over a dining area. The soft and flattering flicker of candlelight creates a gentle ambience.

## HEATING AND COOKING

Freestanding outdoor heaters have become increasingly popular because they extend the amount of time that can be spent outside on the patio or deck, especially early in the season and later in autumn. A range of patio heaters powered by bottled gas is available; they are designed to take the edge off the chill evening air by directing heat from head-height into a very local area. Braziers fuelled by smokeless barbecue coals perform a similar function.

Outdoor cooking seems to provide a focus for conversation. It is important, therefore, to choose a model that suits your cooking skills, and garden space, from the many charcoal- or gas-powered barbecues to one of the new generation of decorative garden stoves. These include compact, wood-fired terracotta ovens, which are shaped like

> Outdoor cooking provides a focus for conversation

beehives and cook by radiant heat, and the kiln-fired, Mexican-style, chimney oven. Mobile barbecues and heaters are very versatile, since they can be moved or turned to overcome problems caused by changing wind direction, rain showers, or smoke.

## HERBS AND FRAGRANT PLANTS

One of the advantages of cooking outdoors is that some of the natural food flavourings can be kept close at hand. Culinary herbs,

▲ MOVEABLE MEALS
*If different areas of your garden are in sun at different times of the day, a portable picnic bench may be a practical option. It is much easier to move around the garden than a set of individual tables and chairs.*

▶ MODERN AND MOBILE
*This stainless steel barbecue has a clean, modern design and is very practical. It is charcoal-fired and easily moved if smoke starts to blow in the wrong direction.*

◄ HEAT OF THE NIGHT
*Gas heaters are designed to take the edge off the chill evening air so that more time can be spent outside.*

▼ CITRONELLA CANDLES
*Insects can often be a problem outdoors. Lanterns or candles that burn insect-repelling oils, like citronella, will ward them off.*

such as basil, bay, mint, parsley, rosemary, and thyme can all be grown close to the barbecue area and used fresh to flavour or garnish cold or cooked dishes. It is also useful to keep a potted *Aloe vera* plant nearby in summer; small sections of its fleshy leaves are very useful for treating minor burns caused during cooking, by smearing the sap over the affected area.

Scented plants like jasmine and lavender are wonderful for providing a subtle fragrance on a warm evening when planted close to a seating area. Other plants make excellent insect repellents: tansy and pennyroyal are particularly useful for driving away those annoying visitors on a balmy summer's evening. If the area is to be used a lot at night, consider fragrant plants that flower only at night (*see box, p.21*).

The benefit of any of these plants, however, is lost if they are positioned too low, or too far away from, the sitting and dining area, and the answer to the problem is to lift them up in raised beds or containers. A raised bed, up to about 75cm (30in) above ground level, will bring the plants much closer, and the edges of these beds make useful arm rests or improvised seats. Raising the plants also makes it easier to look after them, especially for anyone with mobility problems.

## USEFUL PLANTS

*Aloe vera* Spiky succulent with thick, fleshy leaves filled with a soothing sap.
*Lavender* (*Lavandula angustifolia*) Low, grey-green shrub; scented, purple summer flowers.
*Parsley* (*Petroselinum crispum*) Clumping herb with distinctively flavoured leaves.
*Pennyroyal* (*Mentha pulegium*) Spreading herb; aromatic foliage deters some insects.
*Rosemary* (*Rosmarinus officinalis*) Grey-green shrub; aromatic leaves and lilac-blue flowers.
*Tansy* (*Tanacetum vulgare*) Upright perennial; yellow summer flowers; deters some insects.
*Thyme* (*Thymus vulgaris*) Low, cushion-forming shrub with aromatic leaves and bright purple to white summer flowers.

# A SPACE TO RELAX

RELAXATION IS A FEELING of inner peace and tranquillity, and to bring this to your garden, you need to create a quiet corner or slightly secluded area. Here, you will be sheltered from the pressures of everyday life and surrounded by the timelessness of the natural world. Choose fragrant plants to scent the air and a small fountain to capture the relaxing sound of moving water.

## FURNITURE FOR RELAXING

The garden seating used for lounging and relaxing tends to be a great deal softer than furniture used in an eating area. Soft and natural materials, like cotton or canvas, are supported by a metal or wooden structure. The humble deckchair is a fine example; the seat moulds around the occupant's body, and it is very comfortable. There is a wider choice of colour and pattern available in soft furniture – choose a design that will not clash with the planting.

Rigid furniture can be made more enticing if it has removable cushions or paddings, but these will need to be stored away during wet weather or they will absorb water and start to rot. The main advantage of this type of covering is that it can give seating a dual function: the uncovered seating can be used for dining, while the covers or cushions can be added when it is needed for lounging.

Other types of garden seating are more self-contained, such as swing seats, which have their own framework and awning as well as fabric covers at the back and sides.

---

### The colour of furniture is an important element in garden design

---

Perhaps the ultimate lounger is the hammock, either held within a purpose-built frame or hung between two fixed points, such as stout posts or trees. These also have the advantage of being very light and extremely easy to store.

THE SIMPLE
THINGS IN LIFE
*A hammock is
probably the most
basic piece of garden
furniture you are
likely to come across,
but it cannot be
beaten when it comes
to relaxation. This is
the traditional sailor's
hammock, strung
between two trees;
many other styles
of hammock are
available.*

## WATER AND WIND

The one element that is most commonly associated with a tranquil garden is water, and water features are always a good focal point in even the smallest garden. The soothing sound that water makes when it falls over stones or back into a pool can be very therapeutic, and this sound can vary greatly, depending on the type of feature, how and where it has been constructed, and the speed at which the water is running. Usually, the slower the water flow and the shorter the fall distance of the water, the softer and more relaxing is the sound of splashing.

Water features range from bubbling pools or wall-mounted fountains to streams and ponds, and – if the room is available – a swimming pool. More and more people are finding space to fit an outdoor spa, hot tub, or jacuzzi as a watery source of relaxation. These installations can be partially raised out of a deck or patio, so major construction work is not an absolute necessity.

▲ TRANQUIL CORNER
*This wall reflects both the sun's heat and the gentle sound of running water on to a secluded patio.*

▼ POOLSIDE PATIO
*The patio around this pool is a sun trap – ideal for sun loungers. The colour of the paving is picked up by the cushions.*

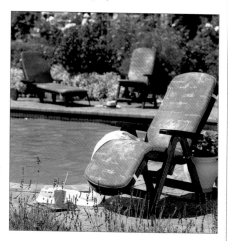

▶ ESSENTIAL FRAGRANCE
*Sprigs of common lavender release an exquisite scent, used in aromatherapy and high-quality perfumes.*

▼ MUSIC OF THE WIND
*The random notes of a wind chime cast a musical spell on a garden.*

Many gardeners find the sound of the breeze relaxing. Wind chimes come in a range of materials, shapes, and sizes, and "tunes"; it should be borne in mind, however, that some people find their gentle tinkling very irritating after a while.

### SPECIAL RETREATS

A relaxed atmosphere in which to sit and read or simply to enjoy the garden and its surroundings can be created under a gazebo or arbour. Arbours are more open structures, and they are particularly good if you really do want to sit among your plants. The entire structure can be draped with climbers, such as roses or honeysuckles, which have been trained over the roof and sides to provide a marvellous atmosphere of dappled shade and natural fragrances. A well-chosen mix of flowering plants will bloom from spring well into autumn.

A more elaborate garden retreat with a roof and solid or partial walls, such as a gazebo or summer house, may have a more utilitarian use in the colder months when the weather can be uninviting. Then they become storage areas for outdoor furniture or mobile barbecues (*see pp.28–29*).

---

## An arbour can be draped with climbers, such as roses and jasmines

---

Children often try to create their own retreat, and although much of their play activity may involve expending a great deal of sound and energy, especially when several are playing together, there will also be times when they prefer to play quietly. Sandpits and play pens are ideal for young children, and they do like hideaways or playhouses of their own. Here, scale is important; they enjoy places that are too small for adults to invade. Fold-away structures are increasingly popular, such as fabric tunnels and tents. These are perfect when the weather is changeable, as they provide somewhere sheltered to play. They are light and collapsible and can be put up by the children themselves.

## A Fragrant Lawn

The most versatile area of the garden is the lawn, which may be used for games, relaxation, or just as an open area for all of the family to share. For such general use, a tough, hard-wearing turf that contains rye grasses is ideal. The lawn need not be restricted to grass; other ground-hugging plants, such as chamomile or thyme, may be used as an aromatic alternative. These plants release a sweet fragrance when crushed underfoot, but they are intolerant of heavy use. The non-flowering chamomile (*Chamaemelum nobile* 'Treneague') is suitable for lawns, as are the creeping thymes, such as *Thymus serpyllum* 'Annie Hall'.

## PLANTS FOR AN ARBOUR

*Clematis* 'Elsa Späth' Blue summer flowers.
*Eccremocarpus scaber* (Chilean glory flower) Brilliant, orange-red flowers in summer.
*Humulus lupulus* 'Aureus' (Golden hop) Beautiful, golden-green foliage all season.
*Jasminum officinale* (Common jasmine) White scented flowers from early summer to autumn.
*Rosa* 'Golden Showers' Fragrant, clear yellow flowers from summer to autumn.
*Wisteria floribunda* 'Alba' (Japanese wisteria) White flowers in spring or early summer.

▲ SOLAR POWER
*Solar technology is a practical and safe alternative to mains electricity in the garden. This floating water fountain is powered entirely by the sun's energy.*

◀ INSTANT CALM
*A swinging bench with its own awning is a wonderful aid to relaxation. Its gentle movement induces a feeling of calmness and even sleep.*

# TYPES OF COVER AND SHELTER

SHADE AND SHELTER ARE JUST AS IMPORTANT as open spaces in the garden. Whether they offer protection from the elements, such as hot summer sun, chilly breezes, or rain, or if they are used to create a secluded retreat away from prying eyes, there are a number of temporary or permanent structures that you can use in the garden. Thoughtfully placed, these structures can be attractive, and they will heighten your garden's design.

### TYPES OF TEMPORARY COVER
There will be times when your enjoyment of the garden is impeded by strong sun, which can damage skin irreversibly, or by rain. As a result, there is an increased tendency to use some type of cover in the garden to provide the necessary shelter.

For many gardens, umbrellas of various shapes, sizes, and colours are often the easiest option, but if a fixed structure is close by, such as a wall or fence, an awning is fairly easy to erect (*see pp.50–51*) and can be used to very good effect. The advantages of these types of temporary cover rest mainly with their flexibility;

the best ones take up very little storage space, and they can be folded up, opened, and erected easily and quickly.

### PERMANENT SHELTER
Gazebos, pergolas, glass conservatories, and arbours all offer shelter in one form or another. A conservatory allows the garden to be enjoyed in cold or stormy weather, but you may need to fit shades if you want

LIFE'S A BREEZE
*This temporary awning, made from an old boat sail, not only shades the garden patio; it also keeps the house cool by shading the windows.*

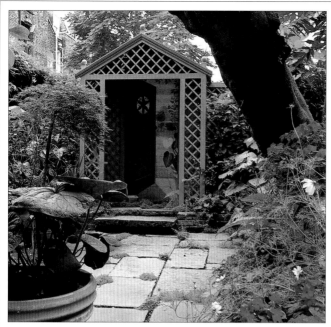

◀ A DEFINED SPACE
*This gazebo provides
a secluded and
sheltered spot in
which to sit and
ponder. Sited
opposite the house,
it gives a refreshingly
different perspective
to the garden.*

▼ SUN SCREEN
*A garden umbrella
or parasol is a
convenient way to
provide a small area
of shade, especially
if it can be tilted
to follow the sun.*

to stay cool through the summer. Instead, you may prefer to move outside and sit under the shade of a flower-clad arbour or pergola, for example.

If your shelter has a roof, like that of a gazebo, it must be angled to allow the run-off of rain water. It also helps if the roof is

> ## Rain shelters must be able to let in maximum light

made of glass or thin canvas, which allows light to penetrate. This is particularly important on cloudy days or in the evening. Failing this, keep the sides of the structure as open to light as possible.

### SCREENS AND SECLUSION
Vertical screens are sometimes necessary to give shelter from wind, to act as a visual screen, or to create a feeling of seclusion and privacy if the area is overlooked. A wall or fence is one option, but a flowering hedge or a trellis planted with climbing plants, such as jasmines or roses, may be far more attractive. Living screens also make the best wind shelters; rather than forming a solid barrier to wind, which causes turbulence, a hedge or trellis is slightly permeable, calming the wind as it passes through, and leading to the creation of a calm, sheltered microclimate.

# LIGHTING THE GARDEN

OUTDOOR LIGHTING HAS CHANGED THE WAY we look and enjoy the garden, and it is greatly under-used. In effect, garden lights extend the time that we can spend outside. When used thoughtfully, lighting will add a new dimension of beauty to the area of the garden that it illuminates, highlighting the best features while the less favourable ones remain obscured in darkness. Practical lights also have their place in the garden, for reasons of safety and security.

## LIGHTS WITH A FUNCTION

Garden lighting will often need to be functional, as a safety feature, to light paths, driveways, or steps, or as a security measure, to deter night-time intruders away from the house. Areas that are used for eating and relaxing at night are simply impractical without a source of illumination, but lighting in these areas goes beyond the purely functional; it can be extremely influential in producing just the right sort of ambience. When choosing a light, you need to consider the design of the feature itself, and the nature of the light that it casts.

Functional lighting that is subtle and decorative can be effective as well as easier on the eye. For example, a bright floodlight may seem like the perfect anti-burglar device, but it blinds the home-owner by casting deep shadows. Rather than deterring intruders, it provides them with somewhere to hide. Most suppliers of garden lighting will offer practical advice.

▲ TRADITIONAL WALL LIGHT
*Less harsh than a floodlight, this type of lighting is probably just as effective at deterring intruders at night.*

◄ THE NIGHT LIFE
*Illuminate the garden with several small and gentle lights to give a greater sense of ambience and a wider area of light.*

◀ SUBTLE YET PRACTICAL
*Discreet lights set into garden steps will illuminate a potential hazard, yet they won't dazzle or blind a passer-by.*

▼ HANGING LANTERNS
*An overhead tree or structure can be used to hang an array of lanterns, but make sure there is no risk of setting the support on fire.*

Path lights can be extremely discreet, especially if they are set into the path itself or into the risers of steps and stairs. It is important that this type of lighting is not too harsh; rather than act as a guide, dazzling lights could cause you to stumble into an obstacle when moving through or

> Outdoor dining areas are simply impractical without lighting

into the illuminated area. Wall-mounted lights that are hidden but produce a soft beam of light directed towards the floor act as a guide without blinding the passer-by.

## DECORATIVE LIGHTING

Well-designed garden lighting brings a special beauty to the garden at night. It highlights the garden's positive features and draws the eye away from those areas we would rather remain unseen.

Many types of decorative lighting employ low-wattage lamps. If these types of lights are positioned in sufficient numbers, with the cables and fittings skilfully hidden, the soft, scattered light they produce can be very effective and attractive.

## NIGHT-SCENTED PLANTS

***Cestrum nocturnum*** (Night-blooming jessamine) Pale flowers perfumed at night.
***Gladiolus tristus*** Creamy yellow blossoms that are intensely fragrant at night.
***Hesperis matronalis*** (Sweet rocket) Delicious evening scent from white to purple flowers.
***Matthiola longipetala*** subsp. ***bicornis*** (Night-scented stock) Pink, mauve, or purple flowers give a spicy scent at night only.
***Mirabilis jalapa*** (Four o'clock flower) Fragrant flowers open in the evening and die by morning.
***Nicotiana alata*** Long and tubular, green-yellow flowers with a strong fragrance open from early evening and into the night.
***Oenothera biennis*** (Evening primrose) Fragrant yellow flowers open in the evening.

▶ LINE OF LAMPS
*This multi-coloured series of lamps is pure decoration, and it livens up the dark shade of this wooden summer house.*

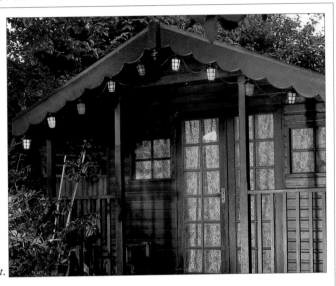

▼ STRING OF BULBS
*A cable of small and white, bulb-shaped lights can be strung through a large tree or shrub for special celebrations. The smaller the lights, the more delicate the effect.*

For areas devoted to seating and dining, the illumination of surrounding walls or screens can produce dramatic, atmospheric effects. Back-lighting uses low-intensity, wide-beamed lights positioned at ground level and directed upwards to provide a wash of light over the wall's surface. Positioned behind pots or furniture, the lights are hidden, yet they create a stunning silhouette.

## Upward-pointing beams create one of the most expressive lighting effects

Lighting from above is known as down-lighting, and it can be a way of imitating nature. Where light is directed through a tree or structure, such as a pergola, it emphasizes their form, suggests filtered sunlight or moonlight, and casts a soft shadow over the ground below. Down-lighting is ideal if the garden has a large, mature tree with a dense canopy.

The direction of light from ground level in an upwards direction is used to highlight an attractive plant, to silhouette

### LIGHTING EFFECTS

• Direct ground-level lights at a blank wall or screen to create soft back-lighting.
• Suggest filtered sunlight or moonlight by pointing a wall- or tree-mounted light through a mature tree or down a wall.
• Use ground-level lights as spotlights to draw the eye to a particularly splendid plant or feature, or to create an intriguing or dramatic silhouette.
• Create pools or rivers of light by illuminating water features, such as fountains or waterfalls. Use purpose-designed, underwater lights only.
• Dot candles or oil-fuelled lamps about to create an instantly intimate atmosphere.

by throwing an outline into sharp relief, or to provide a focal glow in the garden. Up-lighting is one of the most expressive lighting effects for a garden, so long as it is used sparingly.

Subtle lights under the moving water of fountains or waterfalls can create magical effects, as do fairy lights strung around buildings or through trees or shrubs. Such lights are purely decorative, however, and they do very little to increase visibility.

## CANDLES AND LAMPS

Although electric lights are often selected for their convenience, they are by no means the only choice. Oil-fuelled lanterns or torches, and candles of all sizes exploit the gentle and romantic ambience of a flickering flame. The range of styles now available is vast.

The main drawback of outdoor lighting is that it serves to attract moths and other insects that roam around on summer evenings. To keep these creatures at bay, use lanterns or candles that burn insect-repelling ingredients, such as citronella oil.

In areas where people will be in close proximity to candle-type lights, it is vital to consider safety. Naked flames or hot surfaces must be placed out of reach, because they are dangerous to both children and adults. Even passing by quickly can cause some lanterns to flare up and become a hazard.

▶ CANDLE HOLDERS
*There are a huge number of ways to display candles. In lanterns, they can be hung from hooks in brick or metalwork, or they can be contained in ceramic holders or glass tubes to offer protection from wind.*

▼ WROUGHT-IRON TORCHES
*These oil-fuelled torches burn well outside, but open flames are a hazard. They are best avoided where children play.*

# Children's Play Areas

A CHILD'S IMAGINATION IS LIMITLESS, and almost anything has the potential to be turned into a toy or plaything. They will often try to create their own world, and most like to have structures that are too small for adults to invade or where adults are welcome only if they are invited. If you decide to include a play area in the garden for small children, with items like a small sandpit or paddling pool, make sure it is sited close to the house, where it can be supervised.

## How Much Space Is Needed?

For more active play, climbing frames, rope ladders, aerial walkways, swings, and slides are ideal, especially where several of these elements can be combined to provide a multi-activity area. Any of these structures can act as a focus for play, and draw the

children away from other, more fragile areas of the garden. Climbing frames will be much safer if they are built on a soft surface, such as bark chip, of at least 15cm (6in) thick.

Many of the ball games that children play require just a small amount of space. Games like swingball involve a circular area of about 3–4m (10–12ft) in diameter. Basketball can be practised in even less space, as long as there is a wall or fence on which to mount the basket. Both games can be played by groups of children in a relatively limited space, and they can be set up without major work or expense.

## Games on the Lawn

The traditional garden lawn should never be underestimated as a play surface. Not only does it have a cushioning effect when

▲ COVERED SANDPIT
*This sandpit is easily covered and stored away if the lawn is ever needed for a different purpose.*

▶ RUSTIC LOOK
*This wooden climbing frame looks like a pergola; as a result, it fits into the traditional design of this small garden.*

children fall over, but it can be marked and mown in such a way as to form specific play zones, courses, and pitches.

Play structures, of course, do not need to be permanent fixtures. Temporary play structures come in a wide range of designs, such as collapsible or pop-up tunnels and fold-away play houses, which can accommodate up to several children at

> **Even in a large garden,
> children tend to play in
> one small section only**

a time and can be safely put up without adult help. These may provide valuable shelter in changeable weather.

There are also many toys, such as tennis or volleyball nets and basketball baskets, that pack away easily and take up little space when stored. So if a lawn is used by both adults and children, the toys can be moved on and off the area as needed. They can also be moved around the lawn to prevent excessive wear on specific areas.

A BIG ADVENTURE
*A large garden can afford to have a permanent play area for children. This one is built from rounded timber, which makes it safer.*

For young children, the play activity may be more passive, and a shallow paddling pool, a sandpit, or a small slide are more suitable. Small children, however, need constant (if discreet) supervision, so this type of play area must be as close to the house as possible. If you decide to install a permanent sandpit, remember that you could convert it in later years into a garden feature, such as a raised bed.

## CHILD-FRIENDLY GARDENS

If the garden is to be used frequently as a play area, the plant choice must be appropriate.
• Avoid plants that are poisonous or can cause blisters and skin inflammation.
• Avoid trees and shrubs with thorns or spines that may injure young children.
• Plants that attract wildlife, such as birds and butterflies, are a good choice. They will be a source of interest and education for children and adults alike.

# SPACE FOR GAMES AREAS

FORTUNATELY, OUTDOOR PLAY is not the exclusive domain of children; families and friends of mixed age and sporting abilities will often gather together and play or compete on a regular basis. This type of activity usually requires more space than areas dedicated to children's play, mainly because adults are bigger and the number of people involved is generally greater. If most games are to be played on grass, make sure the lawn will withstand the wear.

## TYPES OF OUTDOOR ACTIVITIES

Besides gardening, active garden pursuits vary from games as gentle as croquet or giant chess through to full-blown football or tennis matches. A lawn, although not essential, will be the preferred surface for many of these activities, simply because of its durability and versatility. Also, changes to pitch markings are very easy to carry out on grass when required.

Even games such as giant chess need little planning when played on a lawn; mow it from two directions and at two different heights to create a chequer-board effect on the turf before the game starts. It is even quite easy to create a maze on a lawn. Start by mapping out the required

## SUITABLE LAWNS

• Use a grass type and mowing regime that is appropriate to the games you will play most.
• For ball games such as croquet, you will need a large, level area of fine grass.
• Lay down fine-quality turf for a putting green and cut with a cylinder mower.
• Active games, like football or badminton need a hard-wearing lawn. Opt for a turf that contains durable grass species, such as rye.

THE ULTIMATE GARDEN LUXURY
*An outdoor swimming pool is on most people's wish list when it comes to garden leisure. As a form of exercise, swimming is hard to beat, and, on a hot summer's day, a pool provides a place to cool down and relax.*

◀ GRASS MAZE
*Rather than simply mowing a maze of temporary paths through long grass, the paths can be lined and covered with a thick bed of gravel to make a permanent feature.*

▼ GAME ON GRAVEL
*Gravel is more hard-wearing than grass and involves less maintenance. It is suitable for games such as boules.*

pattern on the grass with sand or bamboo canes as markers, and then mow the pathways through the long grass. The real beauty of making games areas in grass is that all it takes to reinstate the lawn is a sweep with the lawnmower.

## GARDEN SPORTS

For the more dedicated sports enthusiast, a 4–5m (12–15ft) area of closely mown grass can become the perfect practise green to hone golf-putting skills. No specialist equipment is needed, although a really fine finish to the turf does require a cylinder mower, which will cut grass very cleanly;

> Games like volleyball and softball can be played without access to a lawn

if it has a heavy roller, it will also create a striped pattern. To create the hole, a neat hollow can be made with a circular bulb planter. For those less serious about their golf, a few items of play equipment and garden furniture can be arranged as obstacles across the lawn to create an impromptu "pitch and putt" course.

It is perfectly possible, however, to play a whole range of interesting outdoor games without having access to a lawn at all. Games like softball, touch football, and boules can be played on a sand, gravel, or earth surface, and tennis is often played on a range of surfaces other than grass. Volleyball can be played almost anywhere, and cricket and basketball just need a firm surface where the ball can be bounced, such as a patio or driveway.

If you have the space, specialized areas can be set aside for specific games or activities. A permanent tennis court is likely to be the most common example of this, although a swimming pool is probably the ultimate dedicated facility at home.

# SPACE FOR STORAGE

ONE OF THE MAIN DRAWBACKS of making full use of the garden is the amount of furniture, equipment, and toys that gradually accumulates, especially as different items are often needed at specific times of year. Storage areas do not have to be obtrusive or ugly; they can be integrated into the garden's design and even form part of a decorative feature. Look for an unused area in your garden; with a little imagination, it could make an ideal store.

## FINDING STORAGE SPACE

Storage is most important in small gardens that have a multiple number of uses. One way to ease the problem can be to select furniture and equipment that has several functions, such as seats that start out as dining chairs but can be adjusted and turned into loungers. In gardens with a shed or summer house, the solution to a storage problem is fairly obvious: these buildings are relatively waterproof and are often unused in winter, which makes them ideal store rooms.

It can be an interesting exercise to survey a garden and see how many areas of dead space can be found. A space such as the gap underneath a wooden staircase or raised deck – even a cavity of just 30cm (12in) in height and depth – can be sufficient room to store fold-away furniture, gardening tools, sun loungers, or play equipment. Decking that is laid in sections or panels can be adapted to include a removable panel to allow access to a storage cavity beneath the deck.

> It is surprising to discover how many areas of dead space exist in a garden

Any space next to a barbecue could have a door or screen fitted and be used to store the charcoal, bottled gas, grills, and cooking utensils, which will keep them clean and tidy. You could convert a wooden chair or bench into a storage seat by covering the bottom half with wooden panels and fitting a door or lid.

GAPS WITH USES
*These gaps beneath a wooden seating area are home to quite a large amount of dead space. Sliding boxes could be inserted into the gaps, and simple doors fitted to make two weatherproof storage cupboards.*

◄ CLOSED FOR WINTER
*A summer house or gazebo,
as well as being used for
seclusion in warm weather,
can double up as a storage
space – especially for outdoor
furniture – when the garden
is not being used.*

▼ STORAGE BOX
*Purpose-made storage boxes,
whether made of metal or
timber, can be strong enough
to be used also as seats.
Make a feature of a storage
box by surrounding it with
a trellis arbour clothed
with climbing plants.*

## DISGUISING UTILITY AREAS

The most difficult items to store are large
objects in everyday use, which may be too
cumbersome or heavy to manoeuvre from
one position to another. For example,
rubbish containers are generally
unattractive, but they must be accessible.
Some items, such as water and fuel tanks,
cannot be stored; they are fixed in position.
All of these are better unseen, and the
only option is disguise.

A recent development is the camouflaged
refuse bin, which is covered in a printed
design, usually of plants, so that it blends
in with the garden. The most effective
disguise, however, is a living screen, such
as a hedge or a trellis clothed with climbing
plants. Use plants with evergreen foliage
where possible, so that the screen is
effective at all times of the year.

# PROJECTS FOR OUTDOOR LIVING

## AREAS FOR EATING AND ENTERTAINING

CREATING AN AREA FOR ENTERTAINING in your garden can be as simple or as complex as your imagination allows. It may involve laying a patio, building a barbecue (*see below*), making garden furniture (*see pp.34–35*), painting a mural, or decorating a tabletop (*see pp.36–37*). Although some of these undertakings may seem daunting at first, they do not have to be. A good way to begin is to divide your scheme into a number of manageable projects.

## BUILDING A BARBECUE

Cooking outdoors, usually on a barbecue, has become an extremely popular outdoor activity. Portable metal barbecues are quite widely available, but they can be fairly flimsy and reasonably obtrusive in design, and they may need maintenance and storage over winter. It is amazingly easy to construct your own, more permanent, barbecue using some basic building materials.

### PERMANENT BARBECUES

• Fixed structures are the ideal option if barbecues are a regular summer activity.
• Brick or stone barbecues are safer to use. They are very stable and the fire is well contained within three solid walls.
• Fixed barbecues can be made of brick or stone with a grill and grate positioned inside.
• Choose brick or stones that blend with the style of your house, patio, and garden.
• Storage shelves can be built into the design.

THE GROUNDWORK
*Unstable brick walls are dangerous, so always build on a solid foundation. Patio paving slabs make a good base; lay them on compacted hardcore and sand, topped with a layer of mortar. Check that the patio surface is level before building.*

First course of bricks

Paving slabs on mortar base

First course of mortar

Mortar foundation

Layer of sand

Layer of hardcore

Subsoil

◀ BUILT-IN BARBECUE *A solid brick barbecue is stable, safe, and long-lasting.*

**YOU NEED:**
- Approximately 130 fireproof bricks
- Mortar mixed from 2 parts soft sand to 2 parts sharp sand to 1 part cement powder (*see p.70*)
- 12 galvanized metal brackets
- Metal grill plate, 60cm (34in) × 38cm (34in)
- Metal ash tray, 60cm (24in) × 38cm (15in)
- Pencil
- Measuring tape
- Builder's set square
- Ruler
- Builder's trowel
- Bolster chisel
- Mallet
- Spirit level
- Pointing trowel
- Bucket handle tool
- Stiff-bristled brush

# LAYING THE FIRST BRICKS

**1** Mark out the site 60cm (24in) long and 38cm (15in) wide. The open side must face the front, and check the angles with a set square.

**2** Lay a bed of mortar along the outside of the marker line. The mortar bed should be about 10cm (4in) wide and 2cm (¾in) thick.

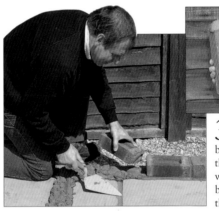

**3** Lay the first course of bricks onto the bed of mortar. Butter the end of each brick with mortar (*see inset*) before laying it. Press the bricks down gently.

# BUILDING UP THE BARBECUE

**1** Half several bricks using a bolster chisel and mallet. Mark the bricks first, and chisel all 4 sides for a clean break. Tidy up the ends of the half bricks with the chisel.

**2** Position the second course of bricks, using the half bricks to create a staggered bond, which creates a stronger structure. Regularly check that everything is in line using a spirit level. Repeat this process for all the remaining courses.

# INSERTING THE GRILL SUPPORTS

**1** **Make sure** that the wall is vertical using the spirit level. Gently knock any misplaced bricks into position, if needed.

**2** **Place 4 metal brackets** between the sixth and seventh courses of bricks. These will support the ash tray.

**3** **Position more** brackets between the eighth and ninth, then eleventh and twelfth, courses. The ends of the brackets should protrude by about 2.5cm (1in).

# FINISHING OFF THE BARBECUE

**1** **Lay the final course** of bricks with their flat surfaces facing up. With a pointing trowel and bucket handle tool, tidy up the lines of mortar between the bricks (*see inset*). Both processes will help water run off the brickwork. Brush off excess mortar.

**2** **When the mortar is dry,** after about 24 hours, slide the metal grill plate and ash tray into place so that they rest on the metal brackets. To vary the cooking temperature, place the cooking grill on either the top or middle brackets.

**3** **The finished barbecue** stands about 1m (3ft) high. The ash tray and grill pieces can be removed easily for cleaning; they should be stored away when not in use.

# ASSEMBLING A WOODEN CHAIR

Wood is a warm and comfortable material to work with, and it blends into the garden well. Many types of wooden furniture are available in easy-to-assemble kit form, so you need not be an experienced carpenter to build them. These instructions are for an armchair with a single seat. All wooden furniture should be treated with a suitable preservative once every year (*see p.76*); a coloured treatment is used here to enhance the look of the wood.

## BEFORE YOU START

### YOU NEED
- 2 arm rests
- 2 wooden dowels
- 2 side panels
- 4 screws
- 4 bolts with washers and nuts
- 4 screw bolts
- Seat section
- Back rest panel
- Wood preservative
- Hammer
- Screwdriver
- Adjustable spanner
- Sandpaper
- Paintbrush

LAY OUT THE MATERIALS
*Check that you have all the materials necessary by laying them all out on the floor. Compare what you have with the list in the instructions.*

### KIT ASSEMBLY
- Take time to read the instructions carefully.
- If any of the pre-drilled holes or joints are too tight, use a drill or sandpaper to increase their size slightly.
- Make sure all screws and bolts are hammered or screwed down tightly so that the heads are slightly below the surface of the timber and cannot cause injury or snag clothing.

## ASSEMBLING THE KIT

**1** **Gently hammer** a wooden dowel into the pre-drilled hole on the underside of an arm rest. Use gentle force only, or you may damage the dowel – if the pre-drilled hole is not large enough, use a drill to make it slightly larger.

**2** **Fit the arm rest's dowel** into the pre-drilled hole on the top of one of the side panels. Swivel the arm rest around, and push its back end into the rebate on the back leg of the side panel. It should be a snug fit.

**3** **Secure the arm rest** to the side panel with 2 screws. The arm rest is now central over the top rail of the side panel. Fit the second side panel in the same way.

**4** **Fix the seat section** to one of the side panels by inserting 2 bolts through the pre-drilled holes. Fit washers and nuts to the bolts, and secure with an adjustable spanner.

**5** **Fit the second side panel** to the seat section with the remaining bolts, nuts, and washers. Tighten all the bolts securely with the spanner.

**6** **Attach the back rest panel** to both side panels with the screw bolts. Start with the bottom 2 pre-drilled holes, and only partly screw in the bolts. Rotate the back panel so the top 2 holes line up, then fit the last 2 screw bolts. Fully secure all 4 screw bolts, but take care not to overtighten them.

**7** **Fully sandpaper** all surfaces to avoid the risk of splinters. Double-check that all fixings are tight before you use the chair.

## PAINTING AND PRESERVING

**2** **Allow the finished chair** to dry for 24 hours before use. Apply a second coat of preservative, if necessary.

**1** **Treat the chair** with a wood preservative (here, one with a blue stain). Do not overload the paintbrush, and follow the grain of the wood with your brushstrokes (*see inset*).

# MAKING A MOSAIC TABLETOP

Mosaic is not difficult, it requires only patience, a bold design for success, and a pair of eye protectors for safety. For the thrifty-minded, it is a wonderfully economic way to use up the odd, chipped, and broken tiles that shops are keen to dispose of. Keep the colour range limited, otherwise small objects like this blue and white tabletop can look too busy and somewhat chaotic.

## YOU NEED

- Circular wooden tabletop and metal base
- Navy blue, mid-blue, light blue, and white ceramic tiles
- PVA glue
- Strip of lead, the circumference and depth of the tabletop
- 20 × 2.5cm (1in) nails
- Grey tile grout
- Marker pen
- Mosaic tile nippers
- Eye protectors
- Spatula
- Scissors
- Hammer
- Small paint roller
- Sponge or damp cloth
- Soft polishing cloth
- Polish

## PREPARING THE MOSAIC

1 **Draw a simple** design outline, using a marker pen, on top of the circular tabletop. This compass design is composed of triangles and concentric circles.

2 **Cut the ceramic** tiles into small pieces using mosaic tile nippers. Cut rectangles for the border circles and irregular pieces for the central design. Wear eye protectors to shield against flying chips.

## MATERIALS FOR MOSAICS

The small pieces of glass, tile, or stone used in mosaic are called tesserae. Glass and ceramic tiles are obtainable from specialist mosaic suppliers, either by the sheet in single colours or in mixed bags. Use mosaic nippers to break these tiles into even smaller pieces, if necessary. You may wish to experiment with other, more unusual tesserae materials for your mosaic, such as old or broken crockery, mirror fragments, pebbles, sea shells, and even flat-backed semi-precious gemstones. Make sure the tiles and other tesserae are all the same thickness and texture, or the finish will be uneven.

BROKEN MIRROR TILES

CERAMIC TILES

BROKEN CROCKERY

MOSAIC TILES

# BUILDING UP THE MOSAIC

**1** **Using a spatula,** apply glue to the central design. Place pieces of tile onto the glue, leaving a slight gap between each piece. Use the nippers to make smaller shapes, if needed.

**2** **Build up** the surrounding area with more glue and the rectangular tile pieces to make a pattern of circles. When all the mosaic is in place, leave it to dry for a day.

**3** **Wrap a strip of lead** around the tabletop and cut it to fit, using scissors. Secure the lead strip by hammering in nails at 10cm (4in) intervals, and then a couple at each end.

**4** **Apply grey tile grout** (mixed to a mud-pie consistency) over the mosaic with a small paint roller. Clean off the excess with a sponge or damp cloth and leave to dry.

FINISHED TABLETOP
*When dry, polish the surface of the mosaic with a soft cloth and fix the tabletop to the table base. This design was inspired by a seafarer's compass, a strong motif in a variety of cool, nautical blues. As a result, it would be the perfect perch for a croissant and coffee in the garden, or for a potted plant or two in the porch.*

# CREATING ATMOSPHERE

A REAS FOR RELAXATION ARE POSSIBLY the most rewarding schemes to create. Lighting and water are two of the most important elements in creating the appropriate ambience, and they can feature in a variety of installations. To begin, concentrate on items that will be the most useful, such as a well-placed outdoor light, and try not to be too ambitious by undertaking major projects that will take a long time to complete.

# INSTALLING A WALL-MOUNTED LIGHT

Garden lighting may be essential for safety or security, and with a little thought, the same lights can be used to create a subtle ambience. Wall-mounted lights take up very little room and can be relatively unobtrusive. In many cases, electric cabling needs to be led across the garden to a light fixture, which is demonstrated in this project. The safest place to bury cable is alongside paving or under a lawn, where digging is unlikely. If you are forced to lay cabling through a frequently dug border, make sure the cable is laid at least 25cm (10in) deep and enclosed by a thick, brightly coloured pipe.

ELECTRICAL WIRING
*Most outdoor lights are powered by electricity, either directly from the mains or passed through a transformer to produce low-voltage current. They are best mounted on a permanent structure, such as a brick wall or stone post.*

Wall socket inside house

Transformer should be sited indoors, close to wall socket

Electric cable should be armoured, especially if it carries mains electricity

Thick, brightly coloured plastic pipe will protect and bring focus to electric cable if it is ever disturbed

Wall-mounted light protected by waterproof cowling and glass bowl.

Conduit through house wall

Wall-mounted light with directional beam

## SAFETY FIRST

• All mains (high) voltage equipment must be installed by a qualified electrician, and the system must be protected by a residual current device (*see p.74*).

• Run electric cable laid underground through a brightly coloured conduit, so it can be easily seen if accidentally disturbed.

• Only use equipment that has been safety-approved for outdoor use.

◀ NIGHT LIGHTS *Lighting set into and above these steps is for safety as well as decoration.*

## YOU NEED

- Brightly coloured hosepipe
- Armoured electrical cable
- Wall-mounted light with light bulb
- Cable grips with nails
- 2 × 6cm (2½in) masonry screws with wall plugs
- 2 bolts
- Spade
- Brush
- Chalk or coloured pencil
- Hammer
- Electric drill
- Screwdriver
- Adjustable spanner

# LAYING CABLE ALONG A PATH

**1** Dig a shallow trench right along the edge of the path with a spade. The trench only needs to be slightly deeper than the paving stones, because you are unlikely to dig this close to the path again when working on the border.

**2** Feed the armoured cable through the hosepipe. This shields the cable and makes it more visible if disturbed.

**3** Lay the cable in the trench. If possible, push the cable just under the lip of the paving for added protection.

**4** Cover up the cable with soil, or turf if the path butts up to a lawn. Remove any dirt on the path with a brush.

# FIXING CABLE TO THE WALL

**1** Clearly mark the exact position of the light on the wall with chalk or a coloured pencil. Use the light itself as a template. Measure out the correct length of armoured cable.

**2** Fix the cable to the wall using cable grips. Where possible, fix the cable along the line of a mortar joint to help disguise its presence. Ensure the cable remains taught.

# CONNECTING THE WALL-MOUNTED LIGHT

**1** Mark the wall to show where the drill holes are to be fitted. Use the back plate of the light fitting as a template. Remove the back plate and make the marks clearer, if necessary.

**2** Drill a hole at each of the marked positions, slightly deeper than the length of the wall plugs. Insert a wall plug into each hole (*see inset*).

**3** Fix the back plate of the light fitting securely to the wall using a screwdriver and 2 masonry screws. Rather than a screwdriver, it will be easier to use the electric drill if it has the appropriate attachment.

**4** The cable must be connected to the terminals in the front cover of the light fitting, then bolt the front cover to the back plate with a spanner. It is always advisable to employ the services of a qualified electrician.

**5** Insert a light bulb into the fitting, then screw on the cowling and glass bowl. Check that the light and armoured cable are both secured to the wall firmly, and that all electrical connections have been approved by a qualified electrician.

**6** Condensation may collect in the glass bowl, which may need emptying and cleaning occasionally.

# MAKING A SOLAR-POWERED FOUNTAIN

Many people are reluctant to install a fountain in the garden because of the potentially hazardous electrical work involved. Solar-powered water pumps, however, require absolutely no involvement with mains electricity, and the risk of shock is negligible. This small fountain is safe to have around children, and instead of glass, a shatter-proof perspex solar panel is used.

## PUTTING IN A WATER RESERVOIR

**1** **Mark out the area** where the reservoir will be recessed into the soil. A 20 litre (5 gallon) container for a reservoir will hold sufficient water to ensure the pump functions efficiently.

**2** **Dig a hole** deep and wide enough to accommodate the reservoir. Remove any large or sharp stones from the sides or base of the hole, since they may damage the reservoir.

### YOU NEED
- Reservoir tank
- Water pump approved for use with solar-powered systems
- Strong wire
- Brick
- Perspex solar panel
- Fine wire mesh
- Plastic sheeting
- Large stone slab with pre-drilled hole
- Pebbles and stone chippings
- Bamboo cane
- Spade
- Spirit level
- Wire cutters
- Scissors

**3** **Loosen the soil** in the bottom of the hole before lowering in the reservoir and seating it into position so that the top is level with the soil. This will allow the soil to settle evenly as the reservoir fills with water.

**4** **Check the reservoir** is level once it is in the hole. Next, pack soil firmly around the sides of the reservoir. This will prevent its sides from buckling outwards and possibly splitting once it is full of water.

# Installing the Water Pump

1 **Attach the water pump** to a brick using strong wire. This will keep the pump stable, reducing vibration and possible damage.

2 **Fill the reservoir** about two-thirds full of water, then lower in the brick and pump. Allow any air trapped in the pump to escape.

3 **Connect the solar panel's** cable to the pump to check that everything works. Adjust the pump outlet so the top is just above the rim of the tank.

4 **Place a piece** of fine wire mesh so it covers the reservoir and 15cm (6in) of the surrounding soil. Cut a small hole in the mesh so the pump outlet can protrude through it.

5 **Cover the mesh** with plastic sheeting or pond liner. Cut a hole in the middle for the pump outlet, and make some small slits to allow water to drain back into the reservoir.

# Finishing off the Fountain

1 **Place the stone slab,** fitting the pump outlet into the pre-drilled hole. Decorate with pebbles and chippings.

2 **Move the solar panel** to a discreet position facing the sun; a series of solar panels will create more power.

# COVER AND SHELTER

MAKING A COVERED OR SHELTERED AREA within a garden can be as simple or as complicated as you wish. The aim may be to construct a simple and removable canopy or awning, which can be put up when needed to give shelter from the sun during the hottest summer days. Permanent structures, such as gazebos, pergolas, or even small summer houses with glazed doors and windows, can be put to practical use throughout the year. These garden buildings can be decorated with an imaginative selection of plants to soften the structure; use fast-growing annual climbers while perennial plants establish themselves.

## ASSEMBLING A GAZEBO

A gazebo is a structure with a solid roof and partially open sides from which to enjoy the garden. Basic kits like this one can be bought from a fence or shed supplier. They are relatively easy to construct, but you must start with a firm, level foundation. Also check with your local authority before you assemble any large garden feature; planning permission may be necessary for structures over about 2.5m (8ft) in height.

The timber in most kits is pressure-treated with wood preservative and pre-drilled with holes for the joints. These instructions are for an octagonal gazebo kit, 3m (10ft) tall and 2.5m (8ft) wide.

A hand screwdriver is acceptable for the job, but an electric drill with a screwdriver attachment is recommended for speed and ease. A secure set of step ladders is essential for work to be done above head height.

Rafter

Finial

Batten

Feather-edged roof board

Roof support

Shaped corbel block

Arched trellis

**FITTING THE GAZEBO TOGETHER**
*Check that you have all the necessary tools and materials before you start, and familiarize yourself with the detailed instructions that come with the kit so you know how it fits together. A minimum of two adults will be needed for assembly.*

Arched timber

Support post

Hand rail

Spacer timber

◄ ELEGANT HIDEAWAY *This gazebo with fretwork panels is decorative as well as functional.*

## YOU NEED

- 8 square posts
- 8 shaped corbel blocks
- 7cm (3in) screws
- 16 angled fillets
- 4cm (1½in) screws
- 2.5cm (1in) screws
- 16 metal angle brackets
- 8 spacer timbers
- 8 roof support timbers
- 1 finial
- 8 rafters
- 9cm (3½in) screws
- 8 battens
- 4cm (1½in) nails
- Pre-cut feather-edged roof boards
- 2 trellis panels
- 2 arched trellis panels
- 2 hand rail panels
- 8 arched timbers
- Tape measure
- Pencil
- Screwdriver or electric drill with attachment
- Spirit level
- Hammer

# PREPARING THE SIDE FRAMES

1 **Mark the position** for a shaped corbel block 4.5cm (1¾in) from the top of each square post using a tape measure and pencil.

2 **Position a shaped** corbel block to the marked line. Secure it in place with 7cm (3in) screws. Repeat for the remaining 7 posts.

3 **Position an angled fillet** along the length of one side of a square post. The steepest face of the fillet should align with the front face of the post (the face with the corbel).

4 **Secure the fillet** in place using 4cm (1½in) screws, then secure another on the opposite side of the post. Fix fillets to the remaining posts in the same way to create 8 support posts.

5 **The finished support posts** have one shaped corbel block at the top of the front face, and angled fillets on either side. Check that all the fixings are secure and safe.

6 **Attach metal** angle brackets to either end of a spacer timber using 2.5cm (1in) screws. Fit the rest of the brackets to the remaining spacer timbers.

7 **Secure the end** of a spacer timber to the base of a support post. Use a 2.5cm (1in) screw to fix it to the angled fillet. Make sure the bases of timber and post are aligned.

**8** **Measure and mark** the relative position of a roof support timber against a support post. This will ensure even positioning.

**9** **Rest the roof support** on top of the shaped corbel block on the support post. Fix it securely in place with 7cm (3in) screws.

**10** **Fix another** support post to the other ends of the spacer timber and roof support to create a frame. Make 3 more frames in the same way.

## PUTTING THE SIDE FRAMES INTO POSITION

**1** Hold 2 side frames upright, and fit a spacer timber between them. With brackets and 2.5cm (1in) screws, first fix the spacer to the base of the frames, then fix a roof support between their tops. The angle of the fillets ensures that the frames are held together at the correct angle.

**2** Add another side frame to the gazebo as in step 1. The structure should now stand without any support.

**3** **Secure the fourth** side frame to the gazebo as in step 1. Use a stable set of step ladders to reach the roof supports.

**4** **Fix the remaining** roof supports and spacer timbers to complete the octagon. Place a spirit level across the top to check the gazebo is level. Make sure that the structure stands solidly and safely, and re-tighten any joints as necessary.

# MAKING THE ROOF

**1** **Mark the finial** 7cm (3in) down on each of its flat faces. Line 2 rafters up to the marks on opposite sides, and fix to the finial with 7cm (3in) screws.

**2** **Lift the rafters** onto the roof support frame so they sit on 2 support posts. Secure the floating ends of the rafters to the roof support frame with 9cm (3½in) screws.

**3** **Work around** the structure fixing the remaining rafters into place. For each rafter, fix the bottom first, then secure the top after lining it up to the mark on the finial.

**4** **Position a batten** down the middle of one of the rafters. Fix it into place by hammering about 7 nails along its length. Work around the roof until all 8 battens are in place.

**5** **Begin to nail down** the feather-edged roof boards. Work on one roof section at a time; start with the longest roof board at the bottom, which should overhang the edge slightly.

**6** **Work towards** the finial, fitting each roof board securely between the battens so that they overlap one another by about 2cm (¾in). Continue until all the roof sections are fitted.

# FINISHING OFF THE GAZEBO

**1** Secure a trellis panel into the rear left side frame with 7cm (3in) screws. Fit a second trellis into the rear right side frame.

**2** Secure an arched trellis into the front left side frame with 7cm (3in) screws. Fit another into the front right frame.

**3** Secure the hand rail panels beneath each arched trellis with 7cm (3in) screws. Check that they are completely level.

**4** Position an arched timber in one top corner of the front side frame. Secure the timber piece to the support post and the roof support with 7cm (3in) screws.

**5** Fasten a second arched timber to the front side frame to complete the archway. Use the remaining timber arches to fit archways on the left, right, and rear side frames.

**6** Remove spacer timbers from front, left, right, and rear entrance ways once the gazebo is fully constructed.

## PLANTING GUIDE

• Grow climbing plants in containers and train them through the trellis panels to clothe the structure.

• For summer shade, use large-leaved climbers such as *Vitis coignetiae*, which also colours well in autumn.

• For winter interest, plant evergreens with attractive foliage, such as ivy.

# PUTTING UP AN AWNING

A simple awning can be an effective shade screen, and it is less formal and easier to erect than an elaborate structure, such as a pergola. An awning made from sail canvas, such as this one, brings a seaside or holiday feel to the garden, and providing a wall or a couple of trees or stout posts can be used to give the required height, very little construction work is needed.

## YOU NEED

- 2 × 10cm (4in) expanding wall hook bolts
- Large canvas awning with reinforced brass eyelets at each corner
- 2 × 4m (12ft) lengths of nylon cord
- 2 × 2.2m (7ft) plastic-coated or galvanized metal posts
- 4 stout tent pegs
- Chalk or coloured pencil
- Tape measure
- Electric drill with masonry bit
- Spanner
- Mallet

## INITIAL PREPARATION

**1** Assemble all the materials required to complete the task. Also double-check that you have all the necessary tools before you start.

**2** Measure the length of the awning against the wall; at either end, mark where the 2 expanding bolts are to be inserted.

**3** Drill holes using an electric drill with a masonry bit. Ensure the holes are the correct depth and diameter for the expanding bolts.

## ATTACHING THE AWNING TO THE WALL

**1** Clean out any loose dust or fragments of masonry from the holes. Insert the expanding bolts (*see inset*) into the holes.

**2** Tighten the bolt fittings with a spanner. Make sure the expanding parts of the bolts are securely locked into place, and the hooks point up.

**3** Attach one corner of the canvas awning to the wall by threading an eyelet through one of the wall-mounted hooks. Attach the second corner.

# PROVIDING SUPPORT

1 **Once you have attached** both corners of the canvas to the wall, check that the awning is tautly held.

2 **Tie the end** of the nylon cord to the third corner of canvas awning. Repeat for the fourth corner.

3 **Secure each cord** about 8cm (3in) below the top of a post. If necessary, leave some space between the post and awning.

4 **Plunge each metal post** deeply and securely into the ground, using the mallet if necessary. Ensure that the posts are straight.

5 **Knock a tent peg** into the ground about 1.5m (5ft) away from each post using the mallet. Angle the pegs away from the post at about 70°.

6 **Loop each cord** around a tent peg, and use a slip knot to tension the cord. If necessary, use the 2 spare tent pegs to stabilize the posts.

7 **The finished awning** should be securely supported by the metal posts and wall-mounted hooks. It can be removed without difficulty for cleaning, easy storage, or if shade is no longer required.

# CREATING AREAS FOR PLAY

THERE ARE FEW LIMITS to the types of play area that can be built for children, and to reach an appropriate final decision, always begin by considering the age and ability of the children concerned, and plan to scale. Toddlers will be at unnecessary risk if they are allowed to use equipment designed for older children, so add more adventurous apparatus as they grow. Seek the advice of your local authority for any specific recommendations or legislation, which you may have to incorporate into the design of your play area.

# BUILDING AN ADVENTURE PLAY AREA

Children love active play, and the more ways they have to swing, slide, and jump the better. Naturally, this type of play is not without risk, so the aim should be to create an environment that makes the children think they are being daredevils and taking huge risks, when in actual fact they are in a safe, controlled play area.

Whatever type of adventure play area is constructed, safety must be the over-riding factor. If possible, use timber with smooth or rounded edges, and make sure that the ends of all bolts, screws, and nails do not stick out – they must be recessed into the timber. To prevent toppling, secure all heavy play structures into the soil with deep ground anchors, and if there is a danger of falling, always soften the play area's surface with a thick covering of wood chips or equivalent. When the structure is complete, examine it thoroughly for potential hazards, and remedy these before you allow children free access; repeat these safety checks regularly.

HOW THE TOWER FITS TOGETHER *Like all kits, this climbing tower comes with detailed instructions. The timber is pre-drilled and all fixings are supplied. A minimum of two adults is needed for assembly, because of the weight of the components.*

Roof beam

Roof section

Floor boards

Floor support pole

Diagonal support

Upright support pole

Side base support pole

Front base support pole

Rope swing

Pre-drilled hole

◄ PROTECTED ADVENTURE *This timber climbing tower and slide is set into a floor of bark chips.*

## YOU NEED

- 1 playtower with slide in kit form
- 4cm (1½in) screws
- 15cm (6in) bolts
- 10cm (4in) coach screws
- 5cm (2in) nails
- 20 × 2.5m (8ft) timber sleepers
- 15cm (6in) nails
- 22cm (9in) nails
- 4 × 60cm (24in) ground anchors
- 15sq m (150sq ft) geotextile membrane
- Felt nails
- 5cu m (150cu ft) wood chips
- Hammer
- Small wood block
- Screwdriver
- Socket wrench
- Spanner
- Tape measure
- Pencil and string
- Marker pegs
- Electric drill
- Builder's set square
- Hand saw
- Sandpaper
- Spade
- Knife or scissors

# ASSEMBLING THE PLAYTOWER FRAME

**1** **Line up** the front upright support poles on the ground. Here, 2 short support poles are placed inside 2 long support poles. Align the pre-drilled holes (*see inset*), and drive the front rung through them to join the support poles together.

**2** **Lift the front section** on its side and ask a helper to support the upper pole while the front rung is knocked firmly into place. Always place a small wood block between the hammer and poles to prevent damage. Secure the rung with 2 4cm (1½in) screws.

**3** **Lower the front section** back to the ground, and align a floor support pole on the inside. Hammer 2 bolts through pre-drilled holes (*see inset*); tighten the nuts with a socket wrench.

**4** **Turn the frame over** and fit the front base support pole to the bottom of the 2 long support poles. Use 2 bolts in the pre-drilled holes, and tighten them with the wrench.

**5** **Turn over the frame.** Position a diagonal support at the front, across the lower half of the long support poles. Secure with 2 coach screws and tighten with a spanner (*see inset*). The diagonal support will strengthen the front section. Build the back section in the same way as the front.

## FIXING THE SIDE SECTIONS OF THE PLAYTOWER

**1** **Lay the front** and back sections on their sides, and ask a helper to hold them in position. Join the sections together at the top by bolting on the left roof support pole. The left roof support pole is longer than the right roof support, because it will eventually anchor the rope swing.

**2** **Position a side** base support pole. This should be in alignment with the front and back base support poles.

**3** **Fit the base** support pole using 2 coach screws. Make sure all of the joints are fully tightened and secure.

**4** **Fix side rails** to the upper half of the side section. Turn over the tower and complete the other side in the same way.

# MAKING THE ROOF

**1** Fit the roof beam to one of the prefabricated roof sections using 4 coach screws in the pre-drilled holes.

**2** Tip both roof sections onto their ends and join the second section securely to the roof beam.

**3** The finished roof should be strong enough to stand freely. It is now ready to be fixed to the tower.

# FINISHING THE PLAYTOWER

**1** Move the roof into place at the top of the tower. Fasten it to the roof support poles with 8 coach screws.

**2** Double check all the joints to make sure that all coach screws and nuts and bolts are fully tightened to protect the joints from excessive movement and wear. Rotate the tower to check the remaining joints.

**3** Lift the tower into its standing position. The structure will be heavy, so enlist the help of at least one other adult. Do not allow children to go near the tower until it is firmly anchored into the ground (*see p.60*).

**4** Nail the floorboards onto the back and front floor support poles. Use 4 nails to secure each floorboard.

# ASSEMBLING THE PLAYTOWER LADDER

1 **Lay out** the ladder sections to make sure you have all the parts and that all the holes have been pre-drilled.

2 **Evenly measure and mark** out positions for the rungs on the ladder poles at 35cm (14in) intervals.

3 **Fit the rungs** into position using a spanner and 2 coach screws per rung. Make sure no screws protrude.

4 **Position the ladder** beneath the back floor support pole at the rear of the tower. One side of the ladder will rest on the back diagonal support.

5 **Fasten the ladder** securely to the underside of the back floor support pole using 2 coach screws and a wrench. The ladder should be strong enough to hold an adult's weight.

# ATTACHING THE ROPE SWING TO THE TOWER

1 **Climb onto the tower** using the ladder; ask a helper to steady the tower. Thread the rope swing through the pre-drilled hole in the left roof support pole.

2 **Tie a knot** in the top end of the rope swing to prevent it pulling back through the hole in the left roof support pole. Make sure the knot is tight and very secure.

# CONSTRUCTING THE PLAY AREA SURFACE

## MARKING OUT

• Allow enough space on all sides of play equipment to prevent children knocking into dangerous obstacles.

• Rather than use a builder's square, which may be too small for large areas, measure right angles with marker pegs, a tape measure, and string. Any triangle with sides measured to the ratio of 3:4:5 – for example, 1.2m (4ft) × 1.6m (5ft) × 2m (6½ft) – will include a right angle.

1 **Measure and mark** out the play area using a tape measure, string, and marker pegs. Check that all corners are at right angles by measuring a 3:4:5 triangle at each one (*see box, left*). Ensure the surface is level, so any play structures will be stable.

2 **Lay out** the timber sleepers along the boundary of the marked-out play area. With an electric drill, make pilot holes for the nails where the joints are to be made.

3 **Fasten the joints** together using 15cm (6in) nails hammered through the pilot holes and into the sleepers. Make sure the nail heads do not protrude from the pilot holes.

4 **Measure and mark** the last sleepers that have to be cut to size. For accurate, right-angled joints, always use a builder's set square.

5 **Cut each sleeper** along the marked line carefully with a hand saw to keep all edges square. Smooth down rough edges with sandpaper.

6 **Position a second** layer of sleepers on top of the first so all joints overlap. Join the top to the bottom sleepers with 22cm (9in) nails.

# PUTTING IN GROUND ANCHORS

1 **Mark the ground** to show the desired position of the base of the playtower. Dig a hole about 38cm (15in) deep at each corner. Leave the dug soil next to the holes.

2 **Twist a ground anchor** into the bottom of each hole using a spanner. Keep twisting until the tip of the ground anchor is firmly embedded in the soil.

3 **Fill in each hole** around its ground anchor with the loose soil. Firm the soil frequently as the hole is filled to make sure that the anchor is well secured.

4 **Once buried,** the hooked ends of the anchors should be protruding at equal heights from the soil so they can be fixed to the legs of the playtower.

5 **Secure ground anchors** are now in position inside the walled play area. Ensure the retaining wall is strong and stable, because it will have to withstand a lot of wear. The play area is now ready to be lined and filled with wood chips (*see pp.60–61*).

# LINING THE PLAY AREA

1 **Spread out** the geotextile membrane so that it covers the entire area inside the retaining walls of the play area. It may be necessary to tack the membrane to the wooden planks to prevent it blowing around while it is being laid. Make sure any joins in the membrane overlap by at least 30cm (12in).

2 **Cut a small slit** above each of the ground anchors to allow them to penetrate the membrane. Try to make the slit as small as possible.

3 **Push the membrane down** so that it lies flat against the soil and the ground anchors protrude through. Smooth out any wrinkles.

4 **Fasten the membrane** to the inside of the retaining wall using felt nails. Space the nails about 30–38cm (12–15in) apart.

# POSITIONING THE PLAYTOWER

1 **Move the playtower** into place so that each of the 4 upright support poles are positioned next to a ground anchor. The assembled tower is heavy and awkward to move, and the membrane can be quite slippery to work on, so this job must be done by at least 2 adults.

2 **Bolt the tower** firmly to ground anchors using 4 coach screws and a socket wrench. Afterwards, check that the tower is level and completely stable.

# FINISHING OFF THE ADVENTURE PLAY AREA

**1** Manoeuvre the plastic slide to meet the floorboards of the playtower. Make sure both ends of the slide are level so it will not twist when in use.

**2** Secure the top of the slide to the tower floor with 2 4cm (1½in) screws. Make sure the heads of the screws do not stick out.

## WOOD CHIPS

• A layer of wood chips 15cm (6in) deep is often sufficient to break a child's fall. Check with your local authority to find out if there are any guidelines or regulations.

• Wood chips are best laid over a geotextile membrane, which excludes weeds, while allowing water to drain away.

• Wood chips are expensive if bought by the bag. A local timber yard may be able to supply a bulk load for a reasonable price.

**3** Spread wood chips over the entire play area. A depth of at least 15cm (6in) should be laid for it to be effective (*see box, right*). The wood chip surface will need to be raked regularly to ensure airborne weeds do not become established and that the heavily used areas retain a full depth of chips. Occasionally, the entire surface may need to be topped up.

**4** The finished adventure play area is now ready for use, and it should last for many years. As a precautionary measure, however, check the stability of the structure and the tightness of all bolts and screws at least once a year, preferably in dry weather. Also smooth any roughened parts of the timber. Cracks will develop along the grain of rounded timber; this is not a defect, it is part of the natural ageing process.

# MAKING A SANDPIT

This 1.2sq m (15sq ft) sandpit is quite simple to construct, and it occupies a very small area of garden space. It is built of industrial-grade plywood, which is light, strong, and weather-resistant, and it has a cover to keep the sand contained and dry, and free from fouling by birds and pets. Once filled, this sandpit will accommodate three young children comfortably.

## PREPARING THE SITE

### YOU NEED
• 4 paving slabs 60 × 60cm (24 × 24in)
• 5sq m (50sq ft) industrial plywood
• 8 metal brackets
• 1.5cm (½in) screws
• Child-safe wood preservative/paint
• 500kg (1100lb) washed sand
• 60cm (24in) rope
• Tape measure
• 4 bamboo canes
• String and pencil
• Spade and rake
• Spirit level
• Mallet
• Set square and saw
• Screwdriver
• Sandpaper
• Paintbrush
• Electric drill

**1** **Measure and mark** a square 1.2 × 1.2m (4 × 4ft). The diagonal measurements will match each other if the area is square.

**2** **Tie string** around the base of the bamboo canes to mark out the square. The string will act as a guide for digging the pit.

**3** **Dig a pit** 40cm (16in) deep, inside the string line. Make sure that the sides are smooth and vertical (*see inset*). Place the excavated soil just outside the pit edges.

## PUTTING IN THE BASE

**1** **Compact the soil** in the base of the pit. If it is difficult to level the soil, cover it with a bed of sand 5cm (2in) deep.

**2** **Lay the paving slabs** at the bottom of the pit, and with a spirit level, check that each one is level as you lay it. If necessary, gently knock the slabs with the handle of a mallet until they are level. Continue until all 4 slabs are laid in a square.

# MAKING THE WALLS

**1** Measure out a section of heavy duty industrial plywood for one side panel of the sandpit. The section should be 60cm (24in) wide by 1.2m (4ft) long. Use a builder's set square to make sure all the corners are accurate right angles. Cut out the first section using a hand saw.

**2** In each corner, about 4cm (1½in) in from the edge, mark the position to which the brackets will be attached.

**3** Measure and mark out the remaining 3 strips of wood to the same dimensions as before (*see step 1*).

**4** Saw carefully along the saw lines to make 3 more side panels. As before, mark the position of the corner brackets.

# ASSEMBLING THE FRAME

**1** For each panel, place one bracket on its mark in the top right corner of the panel and mark the screw holes. Fasten each bracket with 2 screws to form a corner joint.

**2** Join the 4 panels together to form a box by securing the first 4 corner brackets at the top of the panels. Turn the box over and screw in the bottom 4 corner brackets.

# FINISHING THE SANDPIT

1 **Insert the box** into the pit so that it sits just on the edge of the paved floor. If you have laid the paving and made the box correctly, the top of the box should be level.

2 **Smooth off** any splinters or sharp edges on the box with sandpaper to make it safe for children to use. An electric drill with a sanding attachment will make this job easier.

3 **Treat the outer** surfaces of the sandpit with a wood preservative. When the paint is dry, bank up the soil around the sides.

4 **Fill the sandpit** with washed or play sand to within 15cm (6in) of the top. Spread the sand with a rake as it goes in, which will make it simpler to fill the sandpit evenly.

FINISHED SANDPIT
*The sandpit should now have a rim of wood about 15cm (6in) high separating the sand from the surrounding garden soil. If there is a danger of children falling over or onto the frame, mound up soil to the top of the rim and turf over the bare soil with grass.*

# MAKING A LID FOR THE SANDPIT

**1 Measure the dimensions** of the sandpit (that is, the width and length) to calculate the area needed to be covered by the lid – about 1.2sq m (15sq ft). Mark out a section of industrial plywood to just larger than these measurements so the lid will have a lip.

## SANDPIT TIPS

• Young children must be supervised at all times, so site the sandpit within plain view of the house.

• Never use builder's sand for a sandpit. Washed sand is cleaner and softer.

• When building a sandpit, buy more sand than required; it will need to be topped up from time to time.

**2 Cut the plywood** to size with a hand saw, then smooth down all sharp or rough edges on the lid with sandpaper to remove the danger of splinters.

**3 Treat the lid** with the same wood preservative that was used for the sandpit. Support the lid above the ground so that it is easier to reach and paint. Leave it to dry.

**4 Drill 2 holes** about 15cm (6in) apart, centred along one edge. Pass a 30cm (12in) length of rope through the holes; knot the ends to form a handle.

**5 Repeat step 4** to make a second handle on the opposite side of the lid (*see inset*). The lid can be placed over the sandpit when it is not in use, which will keep out rain, leaves, and dirt, and prevent animals fouling in it.

# GETTING DOWN TO BASICS

## PRACTICAL MATTERS

FOR ANY CONSTRUCTION TASK to progress smoothly and to achieve the desired result, it is important to have the right tools and equipment for the job in hand. Just "making do" is never enough and involves compromises that may well lead to inferior workmanship. Gather all tools and equipment beforehand to make sure everything is available; a job can take twice as long as necessary if every accessory has to be searched for and found before it can be used.

### TOOLS FOR THE JOB

Quality tools are essential for construction work, even though the initial cost may be high; they should be seen as a long-term investment. Specialized tools for infrequent use can be hired (*see box, right*). To keep tools in top condition, ensure that they are cleaned and stored in a dry place after use.

Construction tools fall into three categories: woodwork tools, such as saws and chisels; building tools, like shovels and masonry drills; and general-purpose tools, such as spirit levels and hammers.

### TOOLS FOR HIRE

• Some of the most useful specialized tools for garden construction are cement mixers, stone or block cutters, plate compactors, chainsaws, and pneumatic drills; they are available from most tool hire shops.
• Protective clothing and safety equipment can be hired at the same time as the tools.
• Always get a demonstration of how any machinery works before you take it away.
• A good hire shop will offer advice and usually hire by the full or half-day.

PLIERS

SPIRIT LEVEL

BUILDER'S SET SQUARE

STANLEY KNIFE

HACK SAW

TAPE MEASURE

WHAT YOU NEED
*A small selection of basic and general-purpose tools will set you in good stead. They will be useful for a great variety of garden and household projects.*

HAND SAW

◀ DEFINED AREAS *Different equipment is needed to manage different areas of the garden.*

# USING RAW MATERIALS

DECIDING ON WHICH MATERIALS TO USE depends on a number of factors. For example, how long is the structure is expected to last? Ultimately, this boils down to quality and subsequent cost, but it is always good practice to select the best and most appropriate materials you can afford. Safety is also an important factor, especially around children and the elderly. For example, wooden materials should be solidly built and smooth to reduce the risk of injury during use.

## HARD MATERIALS

These are the materials used for long-lasting structures, such as brick barbecues and patios. It is worth taking the time to seek expert advice before making a final choice. Consider the following questions: will the material be damaged by winter frost? Will it be too hot to touch on an average summer's day? Will it crack as it ages? If available, reclaimed or recycled materials can make a new feature look established more quickly, but they can be much more expensive than using new ones.

BUILDING BRICKS
*A wide range is available, but their durability varies considerably. Most types are man-made, although some bricks are natural stone.*

BRICKS FOR GROUNDWORK
*Bricks can be laid in the ground instead of paving slabs, but make sure that the bricks are frost-proof and non-slip.*

PAVING SLABS
*Much solid groundwork is prepared with paving slabs. Choose between natural stone or cast concrete in a range of colours and textures.*

### KEY CONSIDERATIONS

• Heavy garden structures made from hard materials need proper foundations. An unstable structure is dangerous, so seek professional advice and always leave the ambitious jobs to a professional.

• Shifting hard materials – even single paving slabs – is heavy work, so try to recruit a team of helpers.

• Choose hard materials that match and complement the design, colour, and age of your house and garden.

• Ensure that hard materials for outdoor use are totally weather resistant.

# LOOSE MATERIALS

Landscaping and surfacing materials, such as gravel, pea shingle, wood chips, and play sand are described as loose materials, and they are often supplied in bags. Wood chips are popular for children's play areas as they provide a soft landing pad, and they are also used as a garden mulch. Washed sand is used for sandpits, while gravel is favoured for some games areas as well as being a popular alternative to a lawn.

It can be a false economy to choose loose materials simply on the basis of cost. If at all possible, inspect a sample before ordering, especially if you have little experience of the materials on offer. Then only select materials that come from a reputable source. Potentially harmful impurities include sharp stones, weeds, splintered wood or metal, or chemical residues that may stain or burn the skin.

WASHED SAND    SLATE CHIPS    GRAVEL    PEBBLES    WOOD CHIPS

# WOODEN MATERIALS

The range of timber available for outdoor use can be intimidating if you are not familiar with the different types. Most is seasoned or kiln-dried softwood, normally treated with a preservative to extend its useful life to approximately 20–25 years.

Hardwood, such as beech or oak, is less common mainly because it is far more expensive, but it has a greater resistance to rot, lasting up to 30–40 years.

Reconstituted wood, like industrial-grade plywood, is made up of several layers of thin timber sheeting bonded together with glue. This timber offers high strength and durability at a relatively low price.

SELECTION OF TIMBER
*The three main types of timber for outdoor use are softwood, hardwood, and industrial-grade plywood. Try to use products that have been treated with a wood preservative.*

INDUSTRIAL-GRADE PLYWOOD

PRESSURE-TREATED SOFTWOOD

HARDWOOD

UNTREATED SOFTWOOD

# GROUND SHEETING MATERIALS

Many garden construction projects involve the use of ground sheeting, either to retain loose materials, to suppress weeds, or to keep a water feature watertight. The type chosen will be dictated by the situation.

Impermeable membranes are ideal for ponds and other water features, as they are durable and waterproof. Butyl rubber, PVC, and plastic are common examples, available in a range of thicknesses.

Permeable membranes are used to line areas of wood chips, play sand, or gravel. Not only do they stop soil and weeds mixing with the loose materials, but they also allow water to drain away freely. The spun or woven covering membranes are the most flexible, yet they are still very hard-wearing and difficult to rip or tear. Many are designed to last over 25 years.

◄ PVC LINER
*The thickest grades of PVC last the longest. More flexible than plastic.*

◄ GEOTEXTILE MEMBRANE
*Permeable liner that suppresses weeds but allows rainwater to pass.*

◄ BUTYL LINER
*The best watertight membrane; it is very flexible, hard-wearing, and easy to repair (see p.75).*

# MORTAR AND CONCRETE

At its simplest, mortar or concrete is made by mixing sand and cement powder together, then adding some water. Like cooking, however, different recipes suit different occasions, and it is critical to use the right one or the project may lack stability and strength (*see box, below*).

Masonry mortar is used for brickwork, dry mortar is used for pointing gaps in old walls or paving stones, and bedding mortar is used for laying and jointing paving. Concrete is basically mortar with added aggregate (crushed stone or gravel) and is ideal for wall footings and foundations.

Four parts sand
One part cement
Sand and cement mix

**MORTAR MIX**
*Four parts sand to one part cement makes building mortar. Use an equal mixture of sharp sand (for pliability) and soft sand (to bind the mix).*

## MIXING RECIPES

All parts for these recipes are by volume:
**Masonry mortar for building walls:** 4 parts soft/sharp sand mixed; 1 part cement powder.
**Dry mortar:** same recipe as above, but with less water added to make a stiffer mix.
**Bedding mortar:** 5 parts sharp sand; 1 part cement powder.
**Concrete:** 2 parts coarse aggregate; 2 parts soft sand; 1 part cement powder.
**Pouring concrete:** 2½ parts coarse aggregate; 1½ parts sharp sand; 1 part cement powder.

A chemical plasticizer can be added to mortar, which will increase the pliability of the mixture and extend its longevity. This makes mortar easier to use, especially if you are working slowly.

# ORDERING, DELIVERY, AND STORAGE

When ordering materials, establish whether or not the price includes a delivery charge or tax, and whether a bulk discount is available. Find out the size of the delivery vehicle, as this may determine how close to your property the order can be delivered, and ask if the materials arrive loose, which takes up far more room, or in bags. For any deliveries that are to be unloaded onto a public road, it is advisable to notify the local highways department, especially if the goods are to remain there overnight.

Building materials often take up a lot of space, so consider where they are to be stored safely until you use them. Powdered materials like cement, which can absorb water and harden, must be kept in a dry place in sealed, waterproof bags. Bricks and timber must be stored on boards or pallets to keep them off the ground and covered with plastic film to protect them from the weather. Ideally, wood should be stored level and flat to prevent it buckling and twisting out of shape.

## ESTIMATING QUANTITIES

Most suppliers are very helpful when it comes to estimating quantities of materials required for outdoor projects, although they do need a little help. On a sheet of graph paper, mark out the dimensions involved to calculate the area or volume. A supplier can work from these calculations and estimate the quantities of materials required (see below).

| Material | Approximate coverage |
|---|---|
| 36 bricks (laid flat) | 1sq m (10sq ft) |
| 54 bricks (laid on edge) | 1sq m (10sq ft) |
| 45 paviors | 1sq m (10sq ft) |
| 4 paving slabs 60×60cm (24×24in) | 1.5sq m (15sq ft) |
| 100kg (220lb) cobbles of 5×8cm (2×3in) size | 70sq cm (11sq in) |
| 100kg (220lb) loose gravel 2.5cm (1in) deep | 3sq m (30sq ft) |
| 100kg (220lb) rolled gravel 5cm (2in) deep | 1.2sq m (12½sq ft) |
| 100kg (220lb) bedding sand 5cm (2in) deep | 2.5sq m (25sq ft) |
| 100kg (220lb) sharp sand 5cm (2in) deep | 2sq m (20sq ft) |

## A GLOSSARY OF USEFUL TERMS

**Aggregate**
Crushed stone or gravel used as an ingredient in concrete; 20mm (¾in) aggregate is suitable for most concreting jobs.

**Cement powder**
A grey powder that contains limestone. Mixed with water and sand, it forms the bonding agent in mortar and concrete.

**Concrete**
A mixture of sand, cement, and aggregate. It forms a hardened material, which can be used in construction or for surfacing.

**Foundation**
A solid base made from concrete for a wall, building, or other heavy structure.

**Geotextile membrane**
A woven or spun lining material that allows water to pass through it, while simultaneously preventing the penetration of weeds.

**Gravel**
Stone chips derived from parent rock, such as limestone or Cotswold stone, or dredged, water-worn materials, such as fine grit and 6mm (¼in) pea shingle. Available in various grades; used for paths, 12mm (½in) is about maximum for walking comfort.

**Mortar**
A mixture of sand, cement powder, and water. It is used in construction to bond bricks, stones, or slabs.

**Sand**
Soft, or builders', sand is fine-grade; used in mortar, it makes a more binding mix. Sharp sand is coarser and gives mortar a more pliable texture. Washed sand is safe for children's sandpits.

**Shuttering**
A temporary wooden framework to hold wet concrete in place while it sets.

**Wood**
Softwood, such as pine, is often cheaper but less resistant to rot than hardwood, such as ash or walnut, which is sometimes harder to cut. Plywood consists of several thin layers of wood glued together; it is strong and relatively cheap.

# MAINTENANCE, SAFETY, AND REPAIR

SAFETY MUST BE A CONSTANT PRIORITY for any garden construction, from the original plan and building work, right through to the project's completion and beyond, making sure that it remains safe and sturdy for as long as possible. Regular maintenance helps, such as an annual coating of wood preservative or the oiling of moving metal parts (chains, bolts, and hinges, for example), and remember to repair or replace worn or damaged components as they appear.

## PROTECTIVE CLOTHING AND EQUIPMENT

A major proportion of household accidents occur when working in the garden, but many hazards can be greatly reduced. Lift heavy items safely by using the correct posture, or get someone to help with really heavy objects. Never wear loose or flapping clothing, which may catch on moving machinery. Use sturdy gloves to protect hands when working with rough materials, such as bricks or sawn timber. Kneeling mats and knee pads are useful if a lot of kneeling is required, and it is advisable to wear a hard hat when working on a structure taller than 2m (6ft).

### POWER TOOL SAFETY

• Wear eye protection at all times.
• If the equipment creates large amounts of dust, wear a face mask.
• For noisy tools, such as stone cutters or chainsaws, wear ear protection.
• Use circuit-breakers with all electrical tools.
• Do not use an electrical tool during or just after rain, as this may cause faults.
• Always disconnect electrical tools before adjusting, cleaning, or inspecting. Never touch a damaged cable without disconnecting it.

EYE PROTECTORS

HEAVY SUEDE GLOVES

HELMET WITH
SAFETY VISOR

EAR PLUGS

EAR
DEFENDERS

KNEE PADS

RUBBER
GLOVES

# SURFACES AND WALLS

Some surfaces naturally become smooth and even slippery as they age. On steps or ladders, the safest course of action is to replace them once they begin to look worn.

For surfaces that are walked on, a regular scrub and wash with a stiff brush and power hose will remove slippery dirt, moss, and algae. During planning, choose materials with safety in mind. Rather than smooth surfaces, use grooved decking or coarsely surfaced paving slabs to provide the necessary grip in wet conditions, particularly under overhanging trees.

Wooden surfaces, such as fence panels, often have rough surfaces; remove any potentially dangerous splinters with sandpaper. Coat wood every two or three years with a preservative to protect against rot.

Pointing trowel used to push mortar into joints

Buttering tool used to finish off mortar joints tidily

**POINTING TOOLS**
*This buttering tool and pointing trowel are needed to repair joints in brickwork and patios. Use them to apply fresh mortar (see p.70).*

**POINTING A PATIO**
*Chip out crumbled mortar and brush away dust. Soak the area with water, then work fresh mortar into the gaps. Remove excess mortar as necessary.*

**WEEDY PAVING**
*Weeds can be a problem in the cracks of paths or paving. Remove them with weed-killer or by scrubbing with a stiff brush and patio cleaner.*

**LAWN CARE**
*Lawns are important outdoor living areas, so they must be cared for properly. Regularly remove moss, weeds, and dead grass, and keep them mown.*

**NON-SLIP DECKING**
*Wooden surfaces can be hazardous when wet. If the wood is not grooved, add a cover of wire mesh, which soon weathers and blends in.*

## LOOSE SURFACES

• Gravel, sand, and wood chips can be difficult to keep clean. Soil is one contaminant, and it carries weed seeds, which must be removed as they germinate.

• Broken glass is a dangerous contaminant. To be certain of removing all traces of glass, completely replace the loose material in the affected area.

• Unfortunately, pets think sandpits make very inviting toilets. The only effective deterrent is to place a cover over the sand when it is not in use.

# ELECTRICITY AND WATER

THE USE OF ELECTRICAL EQUIPMENT can save a tremendous amount of time, and it can also take away much of the hard and laborious work of construction. Saws, drills, stone cutters, hammer drills, concrete chisels, and a whole range of other tools are now standard equipment available for home use. Take particular care wherever water and electricity are in close proximity of one another, such as in water features. If possible, always seek expert advice.

## ELECTRICAL APPLIANCES

It is always advisable to buy good-quality power tools, many of which are battery powered and incredibly versatile. Other electrical equipment includes items such as garden lighting, and pumps and fountains for water features, which may be run directly from the mains supply or through a device that reduces voltage (*see box, below*). Solar-powered equipment is also available, with a negligible risk of electrocution, although the technology does have its obvious limitations.

RESIDUAL CURRENT DEVICE
*Always use a residual current device (RCD), which cuts off the electricity if there is a fault. This adaptor fits between the plug and socket.*

TIMER ADAPTOR
*It is easy to forget to switch outdoor lights on or off. This programmable timer, which fits into the plug socket, allows for automatic control.*

EXTENSION CABLE
*Outdoors, use a bright, heavy duty, earthed extension cable with watertight connections. A coiled cable is less likely interfere with machinery.*

PROTECTED CABLE
*All electric cabling outdoors must be armoured or protected by an easily seen conduit, for example this brightly coloured hosepipe.*

### HIGH AND LOW VOLTAGE

• For mains (high) voltage electricity outdoors, all cabling, connections, and fittings must be installed by a qualified electrician. The system must also be protected by a residual current device (RCD or circuit breaker).

• Low voltage systems are used in conjunction with a transformer, which should be sited indoors, close to the wall socket. A transformer converts high voltage to low voltage, which presents no danger from electric shock.

• Low voltage appliances have a limited output and are only suitable for small water features or decorative lighting.

• Mains (high) voltage systems are essential for bright lights and large watercourses, but don't forget the RCD.

# OUTDOOR WATER FEATURES

A water feature only looks good when it runs well, which means that the pump must be maintained and cleaned at least once every year (*see below*), and the water may need to be cleaned, topped up, or replaced. Any structures that are part of the design should also be checked; an unsteady rock or brick, for example, is a potential hazard.

Special care must also be taken during extreme weather. Top up the water levels regularly during hot, dry periods. In freezing weather ice expands, which will put great pressure on the liner or water tank. If possible, drain and disconnect the water feature until the arrival of spring; otherwise, use a pond heater and insulate sensitive plants with canvas sheeting.

## WATER SAFETY

• Even shallow water can be dangerous, particularly for small children, who find water irresistible. A barrier, such as a low wire fence or a grill on top of the water (*see below*), can be effective, although it may look unsightly.

• A submersible pump must have enough cable to extend onto dry land. This avoids having to connect cables underwater. All other cables should be kept above water level.

METAL GRILL IMPROVES WATER SAFETY

## MENDING A LEAK

A hole in a flexible liner is relatively easy to repair, like a puncture on a cycle tyre. Most repair kits require warm, dry conditions to get a good contact between the liner and the repair patch, although some adhesives work underwater (*see far right*).

For adhesive tape or repair patches, the liner must first be allowed to dry, then brush the damaged surface clean and wipe with methylated spirit. Cut a patch at least twice the size of the damaged area, and if necessary, cover both surfaces with bonding adhesive. Press the patch down firmly to ensure good contact. Leave for 24 hours, then refill the water feature.

PVC TAPE PATCH

MIXED RESIN

ADHESIVE PVC TAPE

RESIN STICKS

LINER REPAIR KITS
*Adhesive PVC tape must be applied to a dry pond liner. The resin is an adaptable sealant that can be used underwater.*

## HOW TO TAKE APART AND CLEAN A WATER PUMP

Most pumps are fitted with a filter to catch any dirt or debris before it enters the motor, so this filter must be cleaned at least once a year or as recommended by the manufacturer. Switch off the power source, and remove the pump from the water. The outer casing usually opens up to allow removal of the filter and inspection of the delivery pipes and propeller. The motor itself is usually a sealed unit that cannot be opened without causing irreversible damage.

Outlet pipe

Foam filter collects dirt and debris

Motor is a self-contained unit

Strainer excludes large particles

# EATING AND ENTERTAINING AREAS

A GARDEN USED FOR ENTERTAINING usually needs lots of furniture, a bit of food and drink, and as the sun begins to set, some heat and light may be called for too. To prepare, ensure that all food-preparation surfaces are clean and hygienic, check that outdoor furniture is safe and well-maintained, and position barbecues, lamps, and candles completely out of harm's way, especially if children are present. With all this taken care of, sit back and enjoy yourself.

## MAINTAINING OUTDOOR FURNITURE

All outdoor furniture should be wiped down with a sponge and soapy water at least once a year and any upholstery allowed to dry. Wooden furniture will benefit from an annual coating of wood preservative, and metal, or plastic-coated metal, should be checked for signs of rust (*see below*). Always lubricate moving joints well, and in cold climates, store or cover furniture to keep it out of the worst of the weather.

COLOURED WOOD PRESERVATIVES
*Wood preservatives can be combined with wood stains to rejuvenate and protect old or faded wooden furniture.*

FROST-DAMAGED PARASOL BASE
*Winter storage is a priority in cold climates. This water-filled parasol base should have been drained and stored; instead it froze and ruptured.*

## DEALING WITH RUST

Inspect metals structures regularly for any signs of rust or corrosion caused by damage or gradual wear. Remove any loose rust with sandpaper and apply a rust-proofing paint. Always examine plastic-coated metal furniture, play equipment, or tools carefully; any cracks will expose the metal to corrosion, which may be hidden under the plastic.

RUSTY LADDER
*Welded joints and hollow ends of tubes are vulnerable to rust. Sand down the affected area, then treat it with a rust-proofing paint.*

### RUST REPAIR

• The best and cheapest way to minimize rust is to wash and dry metal furniture weekly, and to store it in a dry place when not in use.
• Badly corroded joints and fittings should never be ignored, as they can catch fingers or skin, causing nasty injuries.
• Major rust damage can compromise the safety of a metal structure, especially if it has to bear the weight of a child or adult. If you are in any doubt, get a replacement.

# BARBECUE SAFETY AND EQUIPMENT

Barbecues and garden ovens reach very high temperatures and will quickly cause severe burns when their hot surfaces come into contact with skin; for this reason, wear an apron and oven gloves, and use the correct utensils (*see below*). Keep children well out of reach of any naked flames, heaters, and barbecues, not just when they are in operation, but for a safe period afterwards until they have cooled. The water from a boiled kettle can still injure a child up to 30 minutes after it has boiled.

## FIRE SAFETY
• Always have at least one general-purpose fire extinguisher and a fire blanket close at hand where naked flames are being used.
• Store all flammable materials in a cool, dark, fire-proof place away from the house.
• Where bottles of compressed gas are used as a fuel source, always check any rubberized connections for signs of deterioration or potential leaks, especially after storage.
• Never use a naked flame to test for draughts or fuel leaks.

CHARCOAL   WATER SPRAY   GLOVES

FIRELIGHTERS

NEWSPAPERS

SAFETY MATCHES

APRON   COOKING UTENSILS

BARBECUE EQUIPMENT
*Outdoor cooking requires special equipment. Protective gear for a barbecue chef includes long-handled tools, gloves, and an apron.*

# LAMPS AND CANDLES

Open flames should always be treated with caution and viewed as a potential hazard. As a rule, it is never wise to carry lamps, lanterns, or candles while they are alight or still hot, and they must be kept well away from flammable fabric, such as parasols and awnings, and activity areas – where they may be knocked over. Enclose candles in glass tubes, old jars, or in lanterns. With oil lamps and lanterns, store them empty or with just enough oil present to prevent the wick from drying out. If they become damaged and cannot be repaired by an expert, then they must be discarded.

ENCLOSED   CANDLE IN   OIL LAMP
LANTERN   GLASS TUBE

# INDEX

Page numbers in **bold italics** indicate illustrations.

# ACKNOWLEDGMENTS

**Picture Research** Anna Grapes
**Picture Librarian** Romaine Werblow
**Special photography** Peter Anderson,
Trish Gant, Gary Ombler
**Illustrations** Karen Gavin
**Index** Hilary Bird

**Dorling Kindersley would like to thank**: all
staff at the RHS, in particular Susanne Mitchell,
Karen Wilson, and Barbara Haynes at Vincent
Square, and Dean Peckett at Wisley; Joanna
Chisholm for editorial assistance and Ann
Thompson for design assistance; Gillian
Fountain and Chris Clunn at Loddon Valley
Garden Toys (www.lvgt.co.uk) for supply and
construction of the adventure play-ground;
Andy Christou at Maya Solar
(www.mayasolar.co.uk) for the loan of solar-
powered equipment; Roy Card and David
Dodd at The Outdoor Room Ltd (tel: 01372
742293) for construction of the barbecue; and
Martin Crow at Southern Pergola
(www.southern-pergola.demon.co.uk) for
supply and construction of the gazebo.

**The Royal Horticultural Society**
To learn more about the work of the
Society, visit the RHS on the internet at
www.rhs.org.uk. Information offered includes
plant news, horticultural events around the
country, *RHS Plant Finder*, a garden finder,
international plant registers, results of plant
trials, a gardening calendar and monthly
topics of interest, publications and
membership details.

**Photography**
The publisher would also like to thank the
following for their kind permission to
reproduce their photographs:
(key: t=top, c=centre, b=below, l=left, r=right)

**From the B&Q 2000 range:** 6, 8b, 10bl, 11t,
12cl, 12br, 13tl, 13cr, 15br, 23bl.
**Garden Picture Library:** A. I. Lord 23br; J. S.
Sira 15t; Ron Sutherland 19tl.
**John Glover:** 2, 9tl, 14b, 24br, 30.
**Jerry Harpur:** Brian Berry 28br; Sonny Garcia
9br; Victor Nelson 21cr.
**Indian Ocean Trading Company**
(www.indian-ocean.co.uk): 17bl, 19br.
**Photos Horticultural:** 4bl, 24cl, 25t.
**Ring Lighting Outdoor Range:** 20bl, 20br,
22cl, 22t.
**Steven Wooster:** jacket back tr.